# What Was the Berlin Wall?

by Nico Medina

illustrated by Stephen Marchesi

Penguin Workshop

For Jenn, my favorite Berliner and
Mama Bear for life—NM

For Tom Kostro, best of friends—SM

PENGUIN WORKSHOP
An Imprint of Penguin Random House LLC, New York

Copyright © 2019 by Penguin Random House LLC. All rights reserved.
Published by Penguin Workshop, an imprint of Penguin Random House LLC, New York.
PENGUIN and PENGUIN WORKSHOP are trademarks of Penguin Books Ltd.
WHO HQ & Design is a registered trademark of Penguin Random House LLC.
Printed in the USA.

Visit us online at www.penguinrandomhouse.com.

Library of Congress Cataloging-in-Publication Data is available upon request.

ISBN 9781524789671 (paperback)        10 9 8 7 6 5 4 3 2 1
ISBN 9781524789688 (library binding)   10 9 8 7 6 5 4 3 2 1

# Contents

# What Was the Berlin Wall?

Peter Fechter was born in Berlin, the capital city of Germany, in 1944. That was just before the end of World War II. After the war, Germany was divided into eastern and western parts. So was the city of Berlin. Peter grew up on the east side of the city.

Peter Fechter

When Peter was twelve, his oldest sister got married and moved to West Berlin. Two years later, Peter left school and began working as a bricklayer. He hoped to save up enough money to join his sister in West Berlin one day. There were better jobs there, and Peter longed for a better life.

For many years, the border between East and West Berlin had been relatively open. Half a million Berliners crossed back and forth every day. Twelve thousand children traveled from East Berlin to West Berlin, to go to school. Even the city's subway lines crossed the border.

But on August 13, 1961, Peter's dreams of moving to West Berlin were shattered. Suddenly, a wall was built to separate the east and west sides of the city. It was put up by the East Germans. Now, no East Berliners were allowed into West Berlin. The Berlin Wall separated friends and families. People lost their jobs. East Berliners became prisoners in their own city.

In 1962, eighteen-year-old Peter decided to escape from East Berlin.

Peter's friend and coworker Helmut Kulbeik also wanted to leave. Over their lunch breaks that summer, the two young men looked for places along the Wall where they might be able to escape into the West. In time, they found a run-down factory. It was only twelve yards from the Wall and just might work.

After lunch on August 17, Peter and Helmut sneaked into the building. They planned to wait until nightfall to escape. But around 2:00 p.m.,

Peter and Helmut heard voices in the factory. They decided to make a run for it, even though it was still daytime.

Peter climbed out a small window. As Helmut began to follow, someone entered the room and spotted him. The stranger turned and left without a word. Had they been caught?

Helmut scrambled out the window. Peter and Helmut jumped over some barbed wire. Then they sprinted across the "death strip," the heavily guarded area just before the eight-foot-high Wall.

Without warning, two East German guards began shooting. Helmut reached the Wall. He leaped up and hoisted himself over. Before dropping over the edge, he looked back at his friend. Peter stood frozen, as if in shock.

"Go on with it, jump!" Helmut yelled, before dropping into the West and escaping to freedom.

Peter was not so lucky. A moment later, he was shot and fell to the ground.

A crowd of West Berliners gathered at the Wall. They could hear Peter. "Why aren't you helping me?" he cried out to them. A police officer scaled the Wall and dropped some bandages, but Peter was too weak to move.

Since the end of World War II, American soldiers had been stationed in West Berlin. But now they were under strict orders never to help East Berliners escape. To do so could be seen as an act of war. And no one wanted to start World War III.

The East German border guards could have helped Peter, but they didn't. Soon, Peter was dead. "You criminals!" the crowd, now in the hundreds, screamed over the Wall at the East Germans. "You murderers!"

Four East German border guards took away Peter's body. Journalists snapped photographs, capturing the grim scene for the world to see.

The guards were later presented with a special

flag by Walter Ulbricht, the East German leader. Ulbricht also honored the guards with the title "Best Border Unit of the Year."

Walter Ulbricht

Peter Fechter wasn't the first person to die trying to flee East Berlin. And he would not be the last. The Berlin Wall was barely one year old when Peter was killed. It would stand for another twenty-seven years, and claim at least 140 lives.

Why was the Berlin Wall built in the first place?

And what, in the end, finally brought it down?

# CHAPTER 1
## "You Must Go to Berlin"

Over the centuries, the city of Berlin has had its share of ups and downs. It began more than 800 years ago, around the year 1200, and prospered until a war broke out between European Catholics and Protestants in the early 1600s. Much of the city was destroyed, and its population fell by almost half. But Berlin rebounded by welcoming immigrants and people from different religious backgrounds.

In 1701, Berlin became the capital of the kingdom of Prussia. (Germany did not exist yet.) As the Prussian king grew his army, Berlin grew, too. A grand entrance leading to the king's palace called the Brandenburg Gate was completed in 1791. This majestic landmark still stands today.

Brandenburg Gate

By the 1800s, Berlin had become a magnet for artists and creative people. The lyrics to a popular song at the time said: "You are crazy, my child. You must go to Berlin." Colleges and universities opened, attracting scholars and philosophers from across Europe.

# Karl Marx (1818–1883)

For centuries, Europe had been ruled by the upper classes: royalty and wealthy landowners. The lower class—workers—was paid little and struggled. Karl Marx believed that for society to be fair, there could no longer be classes. He believed capitalism—the system of private land ownership driven by profits, or moneymaking—was to blame for the deep division between rich and poor. Marx thought collective rule by workers and collective ownership of businesses—communism—was the solution. Marx's ideas were considered dangerous and he was banished from France, Belgium, and Prussia. He moved to London, where he died in 1883.

During the Industrial Revolution of the early 1800s, steam power changed Berlin—and the world—forever. Railroads and factories opened throughout the city. Berlin became a center of business and industry, and people flocked there for work.

In 1871, Prussian prime minister Otto von Bismarck announced there was now a united

German Empire. Berlin was the capital of a mighty European power. By 1914, more than two million people called the city home.

Then World War I broke out in 1914. Germany invaded Belgium and France. They attempted a naval blockade of Great Britain.

In 1915, a German submarine sank the passenger ship *Lusitania*, killing 1,198 people, including 128 Americans. The Germans thought victory would come quickly. But the war dragged on until 1918, killing as many as twenty million people. When Germany finally surrendered, it was in ruins. Wilhelm II, emperor of Germany, stepped down, ending five hundred years of royal rule. World War I brought down many monarchies across Europe.

# The Russian Revolution

The Romanov royal family ruled Russia for more than three hundred years. But in March 1917, as World War I raged, the Russian people forced Czar (say: ZAR) Nicholas II to give up the throne. (*Czar* means emperor.) A temporary government was set up to run the country, but Russians were not happy.

In November, Vladimir Lenin, a follower of Karl Marx's beliefs, organized an army of workers, peasants, and soldiers. His army—called the Bolsheviks— captured Russian government

Vladimir Lenin

buildings. They declared Lenin the leader of the world's first communist state. The Bolsheviks established the Union of Soviet Socialist Republics (USSR), also known as the Soviet Union, in 1922.

In 1919, Germany formed its first democratic government. It was called the Weimar Republic, named after the city where its constitution was written. Although Berlin was almost two hundred miles from Weimar, it was the Weimar Republic's capital and center of culture. Artists, scientists, and intellectuals were drawn to the city.

Literature, theater, music, dance, art, architecture, science, and film flourished in Weimar-era Berlin. Albert Einstein won the Nobel

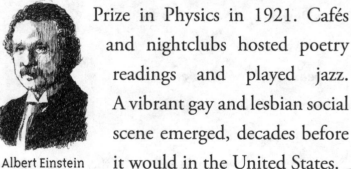

Prize in Physics in 1921. Cafés and nightclubs hosted poetry readings and played jazz. A vibrant gay and lesbian social scene emerged, decades before it would in the United States.

Albert Einstein

Still, the German economy struggled. Crime and unemployment were high. The good times in Berlin—and all of Germany—came crashing down with the Great Depression in 1929.

Adolf Hitler and his Nazi Party wrongly blamed Germany's problems on communists and Jews. Many people agreed with him, however, and the Nazis quickly gained power. Albert Einstein, a Jew, fled Germany and never returned.

When Hitler was named chancellor (or leader) in 1933, his supporters celebrated with a torch-lit march through the Brandenburg Gate. Life in Berlin changed quickly under Nazi rule, as it did all over Germany. Communist groups and other political parties were banned. Freedom of speech and freedom of the press were ended. Hitler's supporters arrested, beat up, and even killed his political enemies.

Jews were hit hardest. Jewish professors lost their jobs, and Jewish businesses were taken away from their owners. German Jews were forced to wear patches showing the Star of David—a symbol of their faith—to identify them to other Germans.

Hitler wasn't content to rule over just Germany. He wanted to take over Europe. In 1939, he invaded Poland, starting World War II. In 1941, Japan—an ally of Germany—bombed a US naval base in Pearl Harbor, Hawaii, bringing the United States into the war.

World War II was devastating. More than fifty million people—and perhaps as many as eighty million—died. The Nazis murdered twelve million people, six million of them Jews.

Berlin—the seat of Nazi power—was bombed heavily by US and British air forces during the war. On the ground, the Soviet Army marched toward Berlin. On April 30, 1945, knowing his war was lost, Hitler killed himself. When Germany surrendered on May 7, the Soviets held complete control over the crumbling capital.

The war in Europe was over. Berlin was in ruins. The question now was: What would happen to Germany and its capital city?

# The Bomb

Even after the war had ended in Europe, the United States was still fighting the Japanese in the Pacific.

For years, the US government had been researching how to build an atomic bomb. In a secret test on July 16, 1945, the first atomic bomb was detonated in the desert near Alamogordo, New Mexico. It created a mushroom cloud seven and a half miles high.

When Japan refused to surrender, the United States dropped an atomic bomb called "Little Boy" on the Japanese city of Hiroshima. It was at least two thousand times more destructive than the most powerful bombs at the time. Three days later, "Fat Man" was dropped on Nagasaki. The bombs destroyed the two cities, and killed more than one hundred thousand people.

Finally, the Japanese emperor surrendered, bringing World War II to a close.

# CHAPTER 2
## An Iron Curtain

Germany was a defeated wreck of a nation. Following the war, it was decided that Germany would be divided up and controlled by the four victorious powers: the United States, Great Britain, France, and the USSR. Eastern Germany went to the communist USSR. Western Germany was split among the other three countries.

Even though Berlin lay in East Germany, more than a hundred miles from the western zone, it too was carved up among the four powers—West Berlin and its 2.2 million residents on one side, 1.2 million East Berliners on the other side. The famous Brandenburg Gate stood at the dividing line, just inside East Berlin, controlled by the Soviet Union.

The four powers agreed to "free movement" among the various parts of the country and capital. This meant everyday Berliners—and soldiers from the four powers—could go back and forth across the border legally and easily.

Postwar Germany, 1945

During the war, the Americans, the British, and the French had teamed up with the Soviets to defeat the Nazis. But after the war, the Soviet Union no longer got along with the Western powers—least of all the United States.

Why? Because the Soviet Union was a communist nation, and the Western powers were capitalist countries. The Soviet Union operated as a dictatorship. The leader of the Communist Party had almost total control. Speaking out against government policies in the USSR could land you in prison.

Soviet Union flag

The Western powers were democracies. This meant there were free and fair elections, where citizens had a say—their vote—about whom they wanted in their government.

The two sides, friends in wartime, quickly became the most bitter foes. Communism versus capitalism. The Soviet Union's allies were now countries in Eastern Europe that also had turned to communism.

During a 1946 speech, former British prime minister Winston Churchill said that "an Iron Curtain [had] descended across the continent." "The Iron Curtain" is how people came to describe the barrier between East and West.

By 1948, the British, French, and American zones in Germany had been combined into one unit. This later became the nation of West Germany. The USSR was furious. West Germany was more than double the size of East Germany!

The United States started giving billions of dollars to help West Germany rebuild after the war. It was important to the United States that West Germany was strong enough to stand up against the communists in the East.

The USSR did not want the United States giving aid to any part of Germany, the country that had so recently started World War II. They would not allow any money into East Germany or the other communist countries in Europe.

The hatred between the United States and the USSR was growing deeper and deeper.

As for Berlin, life was slowly returning to normal. Subway stations reopened. Roads and bridges were rebuilt. But everything happened faster in West Berlin than in East Berlin. West Berlin was like a little "island" of capitalism and democracy in a sea of communism. It had become a thorn in the side of the USSR.

# CHAPTER 3
## Blockade

The USSR had had enough. Joseph Stalin, the leader of the USSR, said that if Germany was going to be formally split in two, Berlin could no longer be considered Germany's single capital. Since Berlin was in East Germany, it should be under Soviet control.

On June 24, 1948, the Soviets blocked land access to West Berlin. No trains, cars, trucks, or boats—no supplies—could come into the western parts of the city.

Joseph Stalin

Stalin hoped this blockade would starve the West Berlin population, and eventually push Western forces out of the city.

US president Harry Truman refused to retreat. "We shall stay, period," he said.

The Western powers responded with what was called the Berlin Airlift. Cargo planes full of supplies landed in West Berlin every minute, twenty-four hours a day.

Some of the planes flew so low that flight crews and people on the ground could wave to each other. Pilots dropped candy and chewing gum attached to homemade parachutes for West Berlin's children. By the end of the blockade, the Berlin Airlift was delivering sixteen million pounds of supplies every day.

During the blockade and airlift, food, fuel, and electricity in West Berlin were strictly rationed. (*Rationed* means people were only allowed to get small amounts of these things.) Fresh fruits and vegetables were hard to come by. The Soviets offered food to anyone from the West who crossed over into East Berlin. But most West Berliners refused.

The Berlin Airlift was working. But shipments of coal would have to increase for the coming winter months. And the two West Berlin airports wouldn't be able to handle all that extra cargo.

In August, construction began on Tegel, a brand-new airport in West Berlin. Bricks and rubble from bombed-out buildings were crushed to build the runways. Around nineteen thousand West Berliners—40 percent of whom were women—worked around the clock to get Tegel up

and running. They came from all walks of life—professors, office workers, construction workers, and scientists alike. By November, Tegel Airport welcomed its first cargo plane.

During the blockade, Soviet forces in and around Berlin outnumbered Western troops by more than 60 to 1. West Berliners feared an invasion.

Luckily, an invasion never came. The Soviets didn't want to risk war with the United States. Not when the United States had the atomic bomb.

On May 12, 1949, after 322 days, the USSR ended their unsuccessful blockade of West Berlin. On May 23, the Federal Republic of Germany (FRG)—West Germany—was founded. A few months later, East Germany became the German Democratic Republic (GDR). The separation of communist East from democratic West was officially complete.

A Cold War was really heating up.

# CHAPTER 4
## Cold War

The Cold War was a new kind of war. There were no battles or bombings. It was a war of ideas: communism versus capitalism. A tense standoff. No one wanted to start another real war, with the United States capable of massive destruction with their atomic weapons.

In August 1949, the Soviet Union tested their first atomic bomb. Like America's first nuclear test, it had been done in secret, at a remote location. The test was a success.

This was the start of a nuclear arms race between the United States and the USSR.

President Truman ordered the development of an even larger bomb—a hydrogen bomb. It was 1,500 times stronger than the bombs dropped on Hiroshima and Nagasaki. In 1952, the United States detonated "Mike," the world's first hydrogen bomb, in the Pacific Ocean. Just three years later, the USSR detonated its own hydrogen bomb.

President Truman

Both sides in the Cold War could now destroy each other.

During the Cold War, the east side of the Iron Curtain was basically a collection of Soviet satellite states. Satellite states are countries that are under the control or influence of a larger, more powerful nation. The so-called "Eastern Bloc" of Soviet satellite states stretched from Poland to Bulgaria.

Many in the Eastern Bloc were unhappy under communist governments. By 1950, more than fifteen million people had migrated to the West. The Eastern Bloc countries responded by tightening their borders.

Nowhere was the departure more dramatic than in East Germany. Between 1949 and 1961, nearly three million East Germans—almost 20 percent of the country's population—had fled.

A large number of the East German refugees were young, highly skilled, and educated professionals, like scientists and engineers. By 1958, East German officials realized they were losing doctors faster than they could train them.

Many left East Germany by crossing into West Berlin. If this "brain drain" of talented East German citizens continued, the GDR would never have a chance to succeed.

What would the GDR do?

# CHAPTER 5
## The Wall

In 1960 alone, the year before the Berlin Wall was built, approximately two hundred thousand GDR citizens fled their country. Four thousand every week. Three out of every four went through West Berlin.

In June 1961, US president John F. Kennedy met with Soviet leader Nikita Khrushchev in Vienna, Austria. Kennedy had stated that the United States wanted peace in Berlin. But during

John F. Kennedy          Nikita Khrushchev

the meeting, the young and inexperienced president hinted that the United States accepted the division of the city—and that the Soviets could do as they pleased in East Berlin.

In private, Kennedy did recognize that Khrushchev would "have to do something to stop the flow of refugees," he said. "Perhaps a wall. And we won't be able to prevent it."

Less than two weeks after Khrushchev and Kennedy met, the GDR leader Walter Ulbricht spoke to reporters. When asked about a state boundary going up between East and West Berlin, he answered: "Nobody has any intention of building a wall."

Ulbricht was lying. With Khrushchev's approval, Ulbricht ordered that the border be sealed in the early morning hours of Sunday, August 13.

Almost no one knew about Ulbricht's top secret plan until it was too late.

Not President Kennedy, who was sailing with his family in Massachusetts.

Not American spies at the CIA (Central Intelligence Agency).

Not even most East German officials.

Willy Brandt, the mayor of West Berlin, was also completely unaware. He was in the city of Nuremberg, more than two hundred miles from Berlin. On Saturday, August 12, he spoke to a crowd about the growing number of East Germans arriving in West Berlin.

"For the first time we shall have taken in 2,500 refugees in twenty-four hours," he said. "The people in East Germany are afraid that the meshes of the Iron Curtain will be cemented shut."

Back in Berlin that night, ordinary citizens began to notice that things were not so ordinary in their city. East Berliners saw more police officers and border guards on the street. Trains entering East Berlin were not returning to the West.

Torch-lit march celebrating Adolf Hitler becoming chancellor, 1933

The Brandenburg Gate after the World War II bombing of Berlin, 1945

Women cleaning up debris from the bombing of Berlin, 1945

Winston Churchill gives his famous "Iron Curtain" speech, 1946.

The millionth bag of coal delivered to West Berlin
during the Berlin Airlift, 1949

West Berliners wave to a US plane during the Berlin Airlift, 1949.

Kennedy (left) shakes hands with Soviet leader Nikita Khrushchev, 1961.

Barbed wire closes the border between East and West Berlin, 1961.

East German soldier Conrad Schumann escapes into West Berlin, 1961.

People flee their homes in East Berlin, 1961.

West Berliners wave to East Berliners, 1961.

The Berlin Wall under construction, 1961

A window in a border building is walled up with bricks, 1961.

US tanks at Checkpoint Charlie, 1961

Two men escape East Berlin through a tunnel, 1962.

President John F. Kennedy walks through Checkpoint Charlie, 1963.

Watchtowers along the Berlin Wall, 1969

President Ronald Reagan makes his famous
"tear down this wall" speech, 1987.

Children draw on the Berlin Wall, 1977.

People climb the Berlin Wall in celebration, 1989.

East Berliners drive through Checkpoint Charlie to West Berlin, 1989.

An East German border guard and a West German woman meet, 1990.

At 1:30 a.m., Sunday August 13, 1961, an order went out to East Berlin's citizen soldiers. Within an hour, twenty-five thousand had joined the guards and police officers at the border. They began digging up the streets and sidewalks to put in fence posts. Asphalt and paving stones were piled up to form barricades. Soldiers laid down miles of barbed wire, then stood behind it, their flashlights on and guns ready.

Sixty-nine of the eighty-one crossing points between East and West Berlin were sealed off over the next twenty-four hours. Eventually, more than six thousand miles of barbed wire would be used to seal off the ninety-six-mile perimeter of West Berlin.

Overnight, neighborhoods were divided. Friends and families became instantly separated. Berliners were in shock.

Some East Berliners tried to take trains into the West. But it was too late. An announcement posted on the walls of the train station read: "Direct [train] lines between the East and West of the city are discontinued."

At first, the "Wall" was still mostly just a barbed-wire fence. So a number of East Berliners still managed to cross into the West. Some swam across the Teltow Canal or the Spree River.

Some East German guards helped people escape—or chose to flee themselves. Conrad Schumann, a nineteen-year-old East German soldier, jumped over the barbed wire into the West. His escape was captured in a now world-famous photograph and movie reel.

After sunrise that first Sunday morning, crowds began to gather at crossing points on both sides of the border. Westerners waved to friends and relatives on the other side of the barbed wire. On the Eastern side, police made the crowds leave, sometimes using tear gas and water cannons.

Protests continued throughout the day across the city, on both sides of the border. By 10:30 that night, four thousand West Berliners had gathered at the Brandenburg Gate. But West Berlin police did not want to provoke a counterattack from Eastern forces. So they pushed the West Berlin protesters back from the border.

Back in the United States, President Kennedy told officials not to issue any strong statements against the new border fence. He ordered that Western forces take no action as the barbed wire went up.

Privately, Kennedy spoke with an aide: "This is the end of the Berlin crisis. . . . We're going to do nothing now, because there is no alternative except war." Because "a wall," he said, was "a lot better than a war."

# CHAPTER 6
## The First Victims

On August 16, the front page of a popular West Berlin newspaper read: "The West Does Nothing!" That evening, West Berlin mayor Willy Brandt addressed a crowd of more than two hundred thousand outside city hall. "We Berliners have something to say to our protectors," Brandt said. "Peace has never been won through weakness."

Brandt wrote to Kennedy, blasting him for remaining silent. He feared if the United States and its allies took no action, the East German and Soviet leaders would further isolate West Berlin. Perhaps even invade it.

Meanwhile, Walter Ulbricht and Nikita Khrushchev moved

Willy Brandt

on to the next phase of their plan. Days after the barbed-wire fencing was rolled out, construction crews began building a concrete wall up to eight feet high. Within a year, more than one hundred watchtowers would also be built.

The Berlin Wall was now complete. But the border between East and West Berlin was not a perfectly straight line. It zigzagged across rivers and cemeteries, and along canals and streets throughout the city.

Bernauer Street and its sidewalks lay in West Berlin, while the apartment buildings that faced it were in the East. Since East German police could not patrol the street itself, they guarded the buildings' hallways and stairwells instead. Some even stood guard *inside* people's apartments! They ordered residents of the ground-floor apartments to turn their front-door keys over to

Aerial view of the Berlin Wall

the authorities, so they could not simply walk into West Berlin.

Police nailed the front doors shut and built new building entrances on the East German side. Residents jumped from their windows in order to escape. West Berlin firemen caught them in rescue nets.

On August 22, the entrance of fifty-eight-year-old nurse Ida Siekmann's building was sealed. She decided to escape early the next morning. Ida did not wait for rescue workers to arrive to catch her. Instead, she threw some bedding out

her window, hoping it would cushion her fall. After jumping from her fourth-floor window, she landed on the pavement, badly injuring herself. Ida Siekmann died before reaching the hospital— the Berlin Wall's first victim.

Two days later, twenty-four-year-old tailor Günter Litfin became the first person shot and

killed by East German border guards when he attempted to swim to West Berlin. The guards who had fired upon Günter were each rewarded with a watch, a medal, and a cash bonus.

One month later, back on Bernauer Street, the East German authorities ordered two thousand people to leave their apartments. For some residents, this was their "now or never" moment to escape to the West.

On September 25, seventy-seven-year-old Frieda Schulze crawled out her window and prepared to drop into a rescue net. But East German officers inside her apartment tried to pull her back. A couple of West Berliners quickly climbed up to grab Frieda's feet to pull her the other way. Caught in a dramatic tug-of-war, Frieda Schulze finally fell into the rescue net, and into West Berlin. Meanwhile, the tug-of-war over Berlin continued.

# CHAPTER 7
## Checkpoint Charlie

Four days after the sealing of the border, President Kennedy decided to send a convoy to Berlin—three hundred trucks loaded with artillery and fifteen hundred American soldiers. The convoy left from its base in Mannheim, West Germany. It traveled slowly along the autobahn—highway—through East German territory.

The United States was sending a message: America stood with West Berlin, and would protect it from communist aggression. By going through East Germany, the US was almost daring the communists to shut down land access to West Berlin—something they had not done since the unsuccessful Berlin blockade.

Vice President Lyndon B. Johnson arrived in West Berlin to meet the convoy. On the drive to city hall, the vice president was greeted by mobs of happy West Berliners.

Lyndon B. Johnson

At city hall, Johnson spoke to a crowd of three hundred thousand. A group of children stood in front, holding up large white letters that spelled out *freiheit*—"freedom" in German.

"The president wants you to know," Johnson said, "that the pledge we have given to the freedom of West Berlin . . . is firm." He continued: "This island does not stand alone."

Meanwhile, the convoy rumbled toward Berlin. Aside from a Soviet fighter plane circling low, there were no threats made to the Americans. By Sunday afternoon, the soldiers arrived in West Berlin to a hero's welcome.

Soviet and East German forces continued sealing the border. On August 23, the number of crossings was further reduced from twelve to seven. Six were for West Berliners and West Germans. Some Westerners had special ID cards and still worked in the East. (But Easterners were not allowed into the West.)

Just one crossing was left open for foreigners: Checkpoint Charlie. It was no more than a wooden shack.

The checkpoint on the East German side was much larger. It featured guard towers, barriers, and a shed where vehicles were searched for hidden escapees.

But Checkpoint Charlie was kept simple on purpose. It delivered the message that the Berlin Wall was not a lawful international border—that these checkpoints were only temporary.

On October 22, 1961, Allan Lightner, a US diplomat stationed in West Berlin, was on his way to a theater in East Berlin. After passing through Checkpoint Charlie, Lightner was stopped by East German guards. They demanded to see his passport. Lightner refused. Only Soviet guards could inspect Lightner's documents. That was part of the power-sharing agreement between the West and the USSR. The East Germans turned Lightner away.

Allan Lightner

In the following days, East German guards continued to deny Americans access to East Berlin. On October 26, the United States sent tanks to Checkpoint Charlie. They revved their engines threateningly. Black smoke rose into the air.

The Soviets responded by mobilizing their own tanks. On October 27, they moved into position. The American tanks were barely one hundred yards away.

A tense twenty-four-hour standoff followed. The world held its breath as the two nuclear superpowers faced off. People worried that the first shot fired would set off World War III.

President Kennedy called Nikita Khrushchev. He assured the Soviet leader that the United States had no interest in invading East Berlin. But Kennedy made it clear that access to East Berlin could no longer be restricted. Khrushchev agreed, and ordered his tanks to withdraw. Minutes later, the American tanks backed off, too.

A terrible outcome had been avoided. In the following years, an uneasy truce settled between East and West. But the Berlin Wall remained.

## CHAPTER 8
## "Ich Bin Ein Berliner"

Over the years, many important leaders visited Berlin. Dr. Martin Luther King Jr. came in 1964. After hearing that an East Berliner had been shot trying to escape that day, King insisted on visiting the site. But US officials did not want him to, and the US embassy in Germany took away his passport. So Dr. King used his American Express credit card as identification at Checkpoint Charlie.

During his sermon at an East Berlin church, King compared the divide between East and West Berliners to the divide between black and white Americans. But "on either side of the wall are God's children," he said, "and no man-made barrier can obliterate that fact."

President Kennedy visited the Berlin Wall in 1963. He delivered a famous speech to a joyous crowd. "Freedom has many difficulties and democracy is not perfect," he said. "But we have never had to put a wall up to keep our people in."

Kennedy concluded by saying: "All free men, wherever they may live, are citizens of Berlin. And therefore, as a free man, I take pride in the words 'Ich bin ein Berliner.'" He was telling the crowd that he was one of them—and that he and free people around the world supported West Berlin.

So what was life like for a typical Berliner? It depended, of course, on what side of the Wall you lived on.

After the building of the Wall, life in East Berlin and East Germany began to improve. Women received equal pay for equal work, and more than 90 percent of women in East Berlin had a job. Housing, jobs, food, education, and health care were provided by the communist government. Crime was low, and the city was safe.

But anything beyond the basic necessities of life were luxuries—things like bananas, chocolate, and chewing gum. Coca-Cola was banned. (Eventually, Pepsi became available.) People waited for up to fifteen years just to buy a car. Apartment blocks were built of plain gray concrete and were not painted. Some apartments didn't have bathtubs or showers, only a sink.

Were all East Berliners upset about the building of the Berlin Wall?

No. In fact, some felt relief. But why?

Before the Wall, many East Berliners had worked in West Berlin. Those East Berliners earned good money and lived better than their neighbors. But most Easterners never had jobs in the West—and so they struggled. Some resented their neighbors who crossed the border for work and earned more. Keeping all East Berliners living and working in East Berlin seemed more fair and equal.

The Wall also made it harder for West Berliners to visit East Berlin. Before, Westerners could easily cross the border to buy goods and services very inexpensively in the East—from gasoline to hairstylists—leaving less for the residents of East Berlin. The Wall changed this.

And not all East Berliners were against communism. Some felt that democracy and free elections had led to the rise of Adolf Hitler. So, really, was communism any worse? One Communist Party member welcomed the Berlin Wall, because East Germans "were trying to rebuild the country. . . . Now we will be left alone."

Still, for years after the Wall was built, older buildings in East Berlin bore scars and bullet holes from World War II. Because of this—and the eerie, quiet streets—many people said that crossing the border from West Berlin into East Berlin felt like going back in time.

Where East Berlin was gray and plain, West Berlin was bright and busy. There were department stores and shopping malls. Grocery-store shelves were full, and there were no waiting lists to buy cars. British, American, and French soldiers organized festivals and put on military parades. Bars and nightclubs lit up in neon played the latest American rock 'n' roll and disco hits.

West Berliners were also free to travel anywhere they wanted. Not so for East Berliners. As citizens of the GDR, they couldn't leave their country without permission, which was very difficult to get.

Freedom of speech did not exist in East Germany. Questioning the way things were could land you in jail. The East German secret police—the Stasi—had spies and informants everywhere. They bugged people's homes and telephones to listen in on their conversations. No one knew whom to trust. By 1989, as many as two million people worked with the Stasi. The secret police kept files on some six million East Germans—one out of every three citizens!

Stasi officers

As in the other Eastern Bloc nations, the media in East Berlin and the rest of the GDR were controlled by the national Communist Party. Newspapers, radio, and television only spread information the communists considered acceptable. Books and movies had to be government-approved.

Western ideas and culture—from the Beatles to McDonald's—were kept out of the Eastern Bloc. For example, in the Soviet Union, to hear the latest hits, people bought secretly bootlegged (illegally copied) records that had been pressed not on vinyl but on old X-rays!

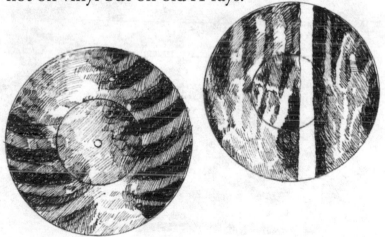

Some people in East Berlin did not know what life was like in the West. Children who grew up with the Berlin Wall in their backyard probably didn't think about it much. They still went to

school, played with their friends, and had family gatherings.

But no matter how high the Berlin Wall got, many East Berliners continued to risk their lives trying to escape to the other side.

## Music at the Berlin Wall

The Berlin Wall inspired many musicians over the years. David Bowie wrote three albums while living in Berlin. In the title track of *Heroes*, he sang: "I can remember standing by the wall, and the guns shot above our heads, and we kissed as though nothing

David Bowie

could fall." In 1987, David Bowie played a huge concert in West Berlin near the Wall. East Germans climbed trees and went to their rooftops to hear it.

Elton John's song "Nikita" is about a man who is in love with an East German guard. "If you're free to make a choice," he sang, "just look towards the west and find a friend."

Before the Wall fell in 1989, East German youth were growing restless. They were protesting, calling on their government for more freedoms. Hoping to ease the rising tensions, East German authorities allowed Bruce Springsteen to play in East Berlin in July 1988. Three hundred thousand people showed up for what became a four-hour concert. They sang along to his hit song "Born in the USA." Springsteen told the crowd: "I've come to play rock 'n' roll for you in the hope that one day all the barriers will be torn down."

# CHAPTER 9
## Higher and Higher

During the Berlin Wall's twenty-eight-year history, more than one hundred thousand escape attempts were made. One East German soldier stole a tank and drove it right through the Wall! Two East Berliners shot a string attached to a cable over the Wall with a bow and arrow, then zip-lined into the West!

One man rented a convertible with his fiancée and her mother. Then, to get the car as low to the ground as possible, he removed its windshield and let some air out of the tires. As he approached the border, he ducked down and punched the gas pedal, speeding right under the checkpoint barriers.

In another successful escape, a railroad worker drove a train full of his friends and family on an old, unused railroad track into the West. Guards had to run out of the train's path as it barreled through the border at full throttle.

Not all escape attempts were made *over* the Wall. By 1964, people had begun to dig seventy tunnels between West and East Berlin. The tunnelers—many of whom were college students— eventually helped some three hundred people reach the West through nineteen completed tunnels. One tunneling project was even filmed by NBC for a TV documentary!

In all, about five thousand people escaped over—or under—the Wall.

Of course, East German officials were determined to prevent as many escapes as they could.

And so the Wall grew. In June 1962, construction began on a second concrete wall, about one hundred yards back from the first Wall. Buildings between the walls were demolished to make room for an open and heavily guarded "no-man's-land" that became known as the "death strip."

In 1965, a new Berlin Wall—ten to twelve feet high—was built to replace the original. It was made of concrete slabs topped with a rounded concrete tube. This made it harder to climb over.

In 1975, construction began on the last Berlin Wall. Forty-five thousand L-shaped segments of steel-reinforced concrete were installed. The slabs were each nearly four feet wide, twelve feet high, and weighed more than three tons.

The death strip became deadlier with each new Wall. Land mines, self-firing guns, and alarms were installed. Three hundred watchtowers were built. Guard dogs patrolled the area on long leashes.

The 850-mile-long national border between East and West Germany also became heavily guarded. Beginning in 1952, a thirty-foot-wide strip of land just inside East Germany was plowed along the entire border. Barbed-wire fences and metal barriers were erected. By the 1980s, more than one million land mines were laid, along with other deadly booby traps.

The East German government claimed that these measures were taken in order to keep Westerners out. But in reality, the border guards' mission was to keep East German citizens imprisoned in their own country.

# "Little Berlin"

Since 1810, half of the tiny German town of Mödlareuth has lain in the West German state of Bavaria, with the other half in East German Thuringia. When Germany was split up after World War II, so was Mödlareuth. A border wall, complete with guard towers and mines, was later built, earning Mödlareuth the nickname "Little Berlin." Today, the village of fifteen households remains divided across the Bavaria-Thuringia state line.

There are two mayors and two postal codes. Phone calls from one side to the other are long-distance. Parts of the border wall and watchtowers remain in place as a reminder of the Cold War.

# CHAPTER 10
## "Tear Down This Wall!"

Over the years, East Germany slowly made reforms. East Berliners who were sixty-five or older were permitted to visit relatives in West Berlin. Many didn't return, but the government didn't care. Older people didn't work, and were a drain on the economy. In 1971, telephone links between East and West were restored.

By the early-1970s, the relationship between East and West Germany had improved. In 1974, the United States opened an embassy in East Berlin.

United States Embassy, East Berlin

Still, East Germany continued to spend billions to maintain its borders. Because it needed money, the East eventually "sold" as many as thirty-five thousand political prisoners to the West for up to $75,000 each. In 1984, East Germany took down more than sixty thousand self-firing guns along its national border in exchange for billions of dollars in loans from West Germany.

Meanwhile, in the secretive Soviet Union, the communist life was falling apart. The economy was tanking. Factories were crumbling. People worried that their great communist experiment had failed.

In 1985, the Soviets chose Mikhail Gorbachev as their next leader. Gorbachev was much younger than previous Soviet leaders and full of new ideas. He did not want to end communism, but he knew it needed fixing.

Mikhail Gorbachev

Gorbachev gave Eastern Bloc countries more freedom. He told them the Soviet army would no longer interfere in their affairs. In 1987, he announced that candidates for important government positions would be elected by the Russian people, rather than selected by the Communist Party.

Mikhail Gorbachev also met with US president Ronald Reagan to discuss nuclear weapons. The nuclear arms race had been on since the 1940s, and the USSR was broke and could no longer keep up. Gorbachev and Reagan liked and trusted each other. They eventually reached a historic agreement to greatly reduce their number of nukes.

In June 1987, Reagan visited Berlin. Despite Gorbachev's reforms, Reagan demanded more action. The people of East Berlin longed to be free, and the Wall needed to go. "If you seek

peace, if you seek prosperity for the Soviet Union
and Eastern Europe," Reagan said, "come here
to this gate. Mr. Gorbachev, open this gate!
Mr. Gorbachev, tear down this wall!"

Erich Honecker was the East German leader at the time. He did not approve of Gorbachev's reforms. He thought things were fine the way they were, and that the Wall would stand for another hundred years!

Many did not agree with Honecker. There were protests across the GDR. In October 1989, when Gorbachev attended a ceremony celebrating the GDR's fortieth anniversary, three hundred citizens began to chant: "Gorby, help us! Gorby, save us!"

Erich Honecker

Twelve days later, Honecker left office. Günter Schabowski, an East German government official, began making daily announcements to the press about changes in East German policy. East German citizens continued to demand the right to travel outside their country without restrictions.

On the evening of November 9, Schabowski was handed an announcement. He read it aloud to the press. East German citizens could now apply to travel abroad without any of the old requirements, he said. Crossing the border between East and West Berlin was now allowed.

When asked how soon this would go into effect, Schabowski said, "As far as I know . . . immediately, without delay."

Schabowski was not supposed to make this announcement until the next morning. He had made a mistake. But when word got out, there was no turning back!

# CHAPTER 11
## Germany United

The news spread fast across the city: The border was open!

But because of Schabowski's mistake, the border guards had no idea what to do. They were quickly overwhelmed by the thousands of East Berliners trying to get through. Luckily, no one was hurt, and the guards soon opened the borders to everyone.

The night turned into a party. West Berliners came to the Wall to greet their friends and neighbors from the East. They climbed on top and dropped to the other side. Families reunited. People took up pickaxes and chisels and began to chip away at the Wall.

Still, most East Berliners returned home that

night. Now that they could move freely between the two sides of the city, they no longer felt trapped. Some found the lights and action of the West too overwhelming!

## Not Before My Sauna

Not everyone rushed to the Wall right away. The night the Berlin Wall fell, a thirty-five-year-old East German physicist named Angela Merkel had other plans. Angela "heard the announcement on television that the borders would open. But it was Thursday, and Thursday was my sauna day, so that's where I went—in the same communist high-rise where we always went." Afterward, she and a

Angela Merkel

friend went for a beer and eventually joined the crowds heading west. In 2005, Angela Merkel became the chancellor of Germany and has been reelected three times.

On December 22, the Brandenburg Gate was reopened. Over the next few months, people continued cutting out chunks of the Berlin Wall. Official demolition began on June 13, 1990. Today, pieces of the Wall can be found at CIA headquarters, the Ronald Reagan Presidential Library in California, and even a casino in Las Vegas. People all around the world keep bits of it as souvenirs.

A section of the Berlin Wall at the
Ronald Reagan Presidential Library

The Western side of the Wall had long been a favorite "canvas" for people to spray-paint graffiti and create art. So a long section of it was left up for artists to paint murals. People still visit it today.

One by one; Eastern Bloc nations began holding new elections and rejecting communism. In March 1990, the Communist Party was defeated in East Germany. On October 3, Germany reunited as one country.

Today, Germany is a prosperous, free, and democratic nation. Its economy is the strongest in Europe, and the fourth largest in the world,

behind the United States, China, and Japan. Berlin is a vibrant and cosmopolitan city—the second largest in Western Europe—visited by millions of people every year.

The Cold War finally ended when the Soviet Union collapsed on December 25, 1991. But the Berlin Wall—and the "people power" that brought it down—will never be forgotten.

# A New Cold War?

After the fall of communism in Eastern Europe, the USSR broke apart into fifteen different countries. Russia was by far the biggest. For a time, relations between Russia and the West improved. But in recent years, under President Vladimir Putin, Russia has once again sought to gain power and influence across the globe. Many Russians like Putin; others do not. Freedom of speech and the press are restricted, and Putin's political enemies are routinely jailed. There is also a great deal of corruption in the government.

Since 2004, Russia has used the Internet and social media to try to influence elections in more than two dozen countries, including the 2016 US presidential election. Russia has also invaded Georgia and Ukraine, two former Soviet republics. And in 2018, Putin unveiled powerful new weapons.

Some people say the world is in a new Cold War. Like the first Cold War, this struggle for influence does not take part on battlefields. The new Cold War is waged mostly online and in voting booths around the globe.

History is made every day, and what happens next is anyone's guess.

# Timeline of the Berlin Wall

1945 — World War II ends; Germany and Berlin are divided among the United States, Great Britain, France, and the Union of Soviet Socialist Republics

1948–1949 — The Berlin Airlift keeps West Berliners supplied with food and provisions during the Soviet blockade

1949 — West Germany and East Germany become independent nations

1960 — Two hundred thousand East Germans flee their country

1961 — The border between East and West Berlin is sealed with barbed wire on August 13; a concrete wall follows days later

— In October, American and Soviet tanks face off at Checkpoint Charlie

1962 — New concrete Berlin Wall built along the border

1963 — President John F. Kennedy visits Berlin

1965 — Taller Berlin Wall, with rounded top, is built

1974 — US embassy opens in East Berlin

1975 — Final, most secure Berlin Wall is built

1985 — Mikhail Gorbachev becomes the leader of the USSR

1987 — President Ronald Reagan visits Berlin

1989 — Border between East and West Berlin reopened on November 9; Berliners begin to tear down the Berlin Wall

1990 — Germany reunites on October 3

# Timeline of the World

1945 — The United States drops atomic bombs on Hiroshima (August 6) and Nagasaki (August 9), ending World War II

1948 — Mahatma Gandhi assassinated in India on January 30

— First Polaroid camera sold on November 26

1949 — The NBA (National Basketball Association) is established

— George Orwell's dystopian novel *1984* is published

— Communist leader Mao Zedong establishes the People's Republic of China

1960 — Nigeria and sixteen other African nations gain independence

1961 — The Soviet Union launches the first man into space on April 12; American Alan Shepard follows on May 5

1962 — First Walmart store opens in Rogers, Arkansas

— The Soviet Union builds missile-launch sites in Cuba

1963 — Alcatraz Federal Penitentiary, aka "The Rock," closes

1965 — The United Kingdom abolishes the death penalty

1971 — Voting age in the United States is lowered to eighteen

1974 — West Germany hosts and wins the FIFA World Cup

1985 — *The Golden Girls* premieres on US television

1987 — Aretha Franklin is the first woman inducted into the Rock & Roll Hall of Fame

1989 — Nintendo releases the handheld Game Boy

# Bibliography

**\*Books for young readers**

\*Burgan, Michael. *The Berlin Wall: Barrier to Freedom.* Snapshots in History. Mankato, MN: Compass Point, 2007.

Buchanan, Rachel, and Oliver Halmburger, directors. *Rise and Fall of the Berlin Wall.* History Channel, 2009.

Garton Ash, Timothy. *In Europe's Name: Germany and the Divided Continent.* New York: Random House, 1993.

Hilton, Christopher. *The Wall: The People's Story.* Stroud, UK: Sutton Publishing Limited, 2001.

Joksch, Reinhard, director. *Berlin, Berlin* (season 1). DOKFilm Fernsehproduktion GmbH and rbb-media, 2005.

Mitchell, Greg. *The Tunnels: Escapes Under the Berlin Wall and the Historic Films the JFK White House Tried to Kill.* New York: Crown Publishing Group, 2016.

\*Otfinoski, Steven. *The Cold War.* A Step Into History. New York: Children's Press, 2018.